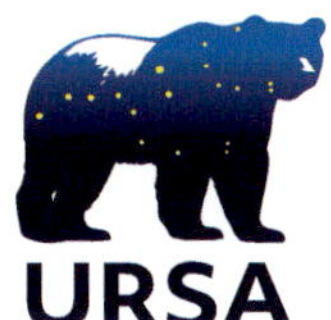

Where You DARE Not Go

Horror Healing

SCARY HOSPITALS AND ASYLUMS

by
Dinah Williams

BEARPORT PUBLISHING
Minneapolis, Minnesota

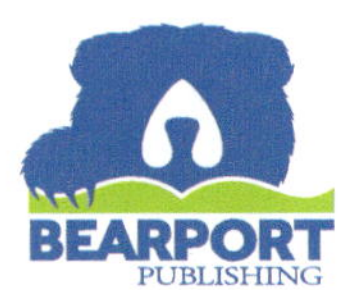

Credits
Cover, © Pablo Caridad/Shutterstock, © Barbara Ash/Shutterstock, © Daniela Pelazza/Shutterstock, © Tanasis/Shutterstock, © KayVonLee/Shutterstock, © Rawpixel.com/Shutterstock, and © grey_and/Shutterstock; 4–5 © Dario Lo Presti/Shutterstock; 6, © Chris Jenner/Shutterstock; 7, © Wellcome Collection gallery/Creative Commons Attribution 4.0 International; 8, © Mwkruse/Creative Commons Attribution-Share Alike 3.0 Unported; 9, © Alfabalık/Creative Commons Attribution-Share Alike 4.0 International and © Bettmann/Getty Images; 10, © Ryan/Creative Commons Attribution-Share Alike 4.0 International; 11, © Carlos E. Santa Maria/Shutterstock; 12, © Wirestock Creators/Shutterstock and © Pandora Pictures/Shutterstock; 13, © Theodor Weyl/Wikimedia Commons; 14, © Willjay/Creative Commons Attribution 3.0 Unported; 15, © Pu Peepu/Shutterstock; 16, © DonViper/Adobe Stock; 17, © dedio/Shutterstock; 18, © Asoep44/Creative Commons Attribution-Share Alike 4.0 International; 19, © Asoep44/Creative Commons Attribution-Share Alike 4.0 International; 20, © Hoapili/Wikimedia Commons and © Eric BVD/Adobe Stock; 21, © Hawaii State Archives/Wikimedia Commons; 22, © Sayed Hoque/iStock; 23, © ChameleonsEye/Shutterstock; 24, © Downtowngal/Creative Commons Attribution-Share Alike 3.0 Unported; 25, © ASDF_MEDIA/Shutterstock; 26, © Crash575/Creative Commons Attribution-Share Alike 3.0 Unported; 27, © Crash575/Creative Commons Attribution 3.0 Unported and © Tawat Kambum/Shutterstock; 28, © Stanley/Adobe Stock; 29, © Finbarr Fallon; 30, © Archives New Zealand/Creative Commons Attribution 2.0 Generic and © Weerachai Khamfu/Shutterstock; 31, © Bettmann/Getty Images; 32, © The New York American/Wikimedia Commons and © Gottscho-Schleisner Collection/Library of Congress; 33, © Everett Collection/Shutterstock; 34, © A. Carty/Creative Commons Attribution-Share Alike 3.0 Unported; 35, © supasart meekumrai Shutterstock, © dannyburn/Adobe Stock; 36, © Royasfoto73/Creative Commons Attribution-Share Alike 4.0 International; 37, © hippix/Shutterstock; 38, © The Library of Congress/wikimedia Commons and © Everett Collection/Shutterstock; 39, © Henry Ulke/Library of Congress and © Channarong Pherngjanda/Shutterstock; 40, © Doug Kerr/Creative Commons Attribution-Share Alike 2.0 Generic; 41, © kanphitchaya/Shutterstock.

Bearport Publishing Company Product Development Team
President: Jen Jenson; Director of Product Development: Spencer Brinker; Managing Editor: Allison Juda; Associate Editor: Naomi Reich; Associate Editor: Tiana Tran; Art Director: Colin O'Dea; Designer: Kim Jones; Designer: Kayla Eggert; Product Development Assistant: Owen Hamlin

Statement on Usage of Generative Artificial Intelligence
Bearport Publishing remains committed to publishing high-quality nonfiction books. Therefore, we restrict the use of generative AI to ensure accuracy of all text and visual components pertaining to a book's subject. See BearportPublishing.com for details.

Library of Congress Cataloging-in-Publication Data is available at www.loc.gov or upon request from the publisher.

ISBN: 979-8-89232-074-0 (hardcover)
ISBN: 979-8-89232-606-3 (paperback)
ISBN: 979-8-89232-207-2 (ebook)

For more information, write to Bearport Publishing, 5357 Penn Avenue South, Minneapolis, MN 55419.

Contents

Creepy Care

Everyone needs care for their body and mind. Hospitals are places where sick or injured people go to become well. Doctors and nurses can help heal everything from small cuts and bruises to serious illnesses and diseases. Psychologists, psychiatrists, and therapists work with patients to improve mental health. They help people using a combination of medications and spoken therapies.

In the past, however, things were different. Some doctors didn't understand the illnesses they were treating. Often, those with mental illness were treated horribly. Many patients died in the care of those who were supposed to help them. It's no wonder some old places that should have been for healing contain horrors still haunting us today. . . .

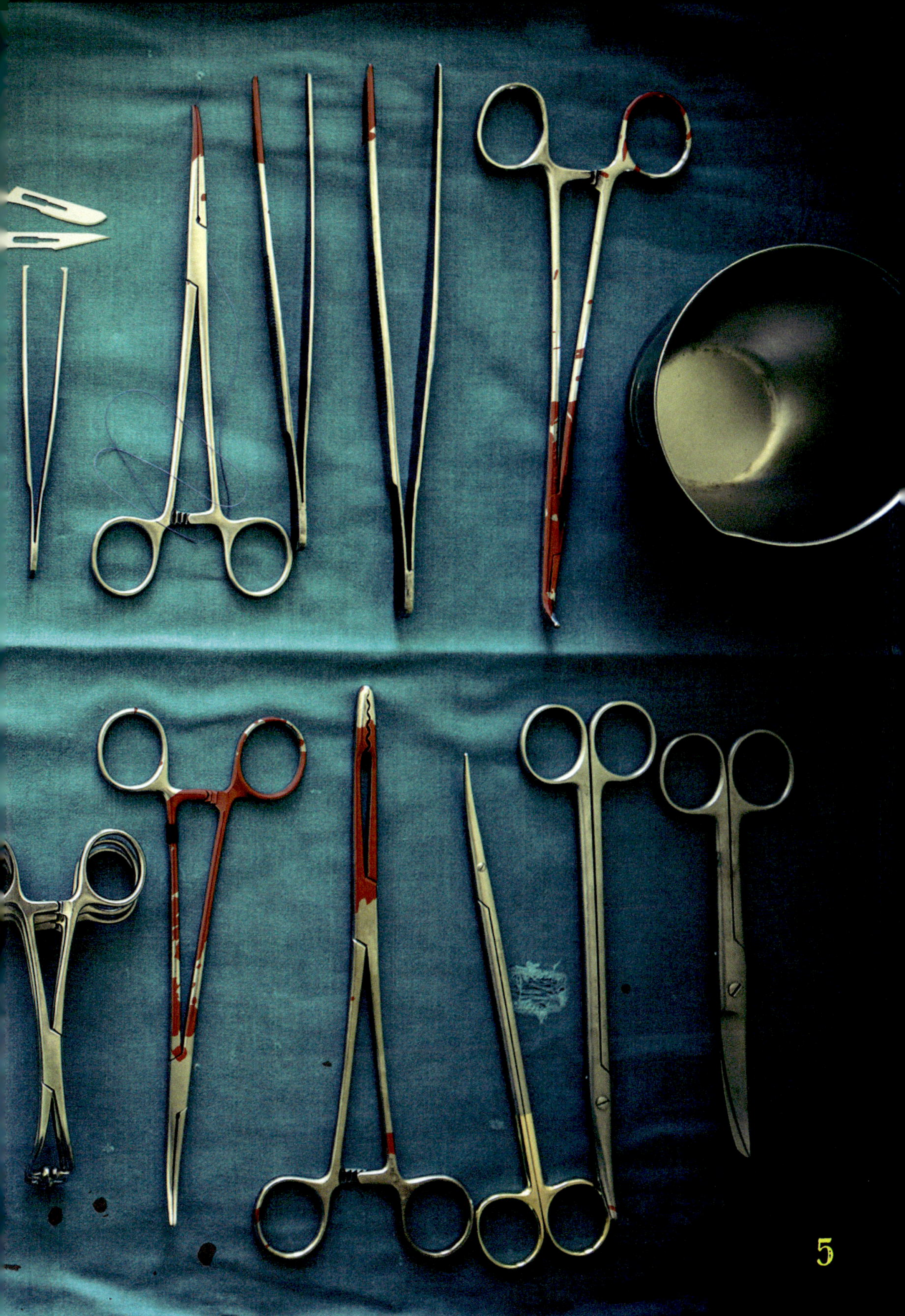

Bedlam at Bethlem

BETHLEM ROYAL HOSPITAL
MOORFIELDS, LONDON, ENGLAND

In the 1700s, many people thought that mental illness was caused by evil spirits. Some doctors thought it could never be cured. Many people with mental illnesses were sent to asylums where they were locked away in cages and treated like animals. For a large part of its history, Bethlem Royal Hospital was such a place.

Bethlem Royal Hospital

The Bethlem Royal Hospital in Bishopsgate, London, began caring for the mentally ill in 1403. Sadly, the care mainly involved chaining patients to the floor or a wall. They were beaten when they couldn't be controlled. By the middle of the 1600s, the hospital was overcrowded and dirty. So, in 1676, the patients were moved to a larger building in a different part of London, called Moorfields.

At Moorfields, the hospital became a tourist attraction. People paid a penny to view and laugh at the mentally ill patients, who were referred to as lunatics. Visitors were allowed to bring long sticks to poke inmates chained in their cells. In 1814, about 96,000 people visited the asylum. The next year, the building had become so run-down that the patients were moved to a new hospital nearby. While this new asylum looked better, the treatment of the patients was nearly as bad.

Patients at Bethlem were often chained to walls.

The word *bedlam* means a place of wild confusion. The word comes from the name of the poorly run hospital—Bethlem. The noise from the patients at Bethlem was said to be so loud, it could have driven a person insane.

A Doctor's Cure?

CHRISTIAN CHURCH HOSPITAL
KANSAS CITY, MISSOURI

Doctors in the mid-1900s would sometimes perform lobotomies. They were said to calm violent patients. In this surgery, a sharp instrument is forced into the brain through the eye socket. The doctor then cuts nerve connections in the brain. Studies later showed that the operation harmed many more people than it helped.

Today, Christian Church Hospital is an apartment building.

In 1927, Dr. Robert Patterson bought the Christian Church Hospital. He was known to be a skilled doctor but not a kind man. For 30 years, he used terrible treatments that he said would cure his mentally ill patients. Some patients were beaten. Others were chained to their beds. If patients could not be controlled, he performed ice pick lobotomies on them. Many suffered permanent brain damage.

In 1957, Dr. Patterson suddenly went insane. All attempts to help him failed. Finally, Patterson's staff used his favorite cure—an ice pick lobotomy. He died soon afterward. The hospital was then sold so it could be turned into apartments. Perhaps people will finally be able to live peacefully in the building.

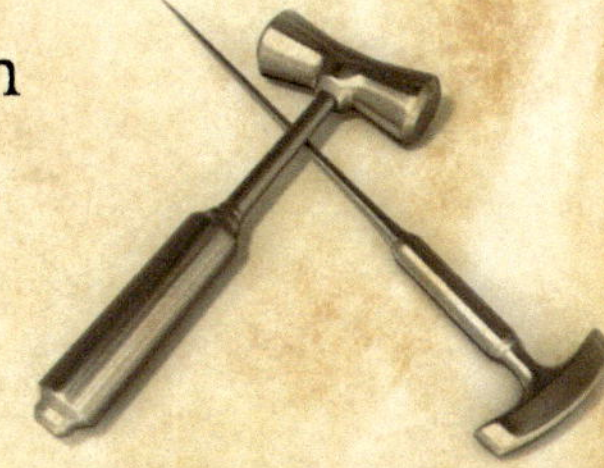

Lobotomy tools

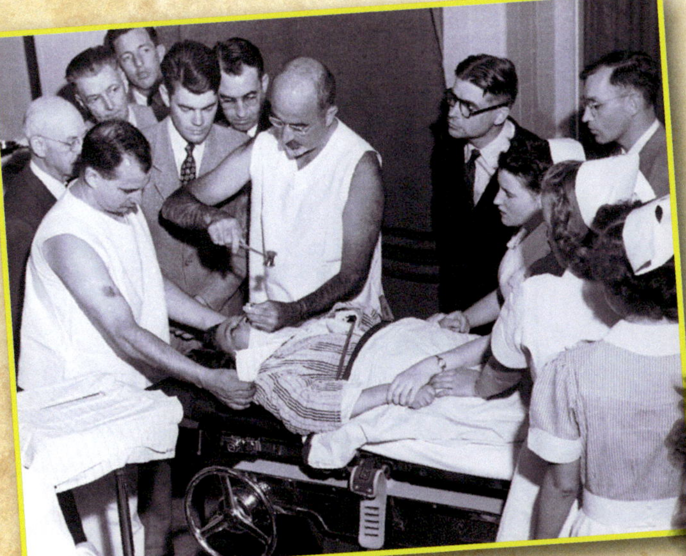

A doctor performing a lobotomy in the 1940s

Between 1939 and 1951, as many as 18,000 people in the United States had lobotomies.

New Hospital, Old Ghosts

ROYAL DERBY HOSPITAL, DERBY, ENGLAND

Hundreds of millions of dollars were spent to build a shiny new hospital in Derby, England. When the hospital was completed in 2009, patients expected to receive the finest medical care. What they didn't expect was a 2,000-year-old ghost.

Royal Derby Hospital

Derby has one of the longest and most haunted histories of all the cities in England. In fact, people report seeing so many ghosts in Derby that it is known as the ghost capital of the country.

The city was originally built on the site of a Roman fort that dated back to 80 CE. The new hospital was constructed over one of the ancient Roman roads that once ran through Derby. Some say that recent work on the hospital disturbed the place where a Roman soldier died thousands of years ago. Does the ghost of that soldier now haunt the hospital's halls?

Several hospital workers claim to have seen a ghostly male figure dressed in a black cloak. He darts between rooms and walks through walls. Many say he is often spotted near the hospital's morgue. Employees are so afraid that those in charge are trying to find a way to frighten the ghost away.

Lionel Fanthorpe, an expert on the paranormal, has found 315 reports of ghosts, werewolves, and vampires in Derby since records were first kept.

Island of Death

POVEGLIA MENTAL HOSPITAL
POVEGLIA, ITALY

Hundreds of years ago, Venice, Italy, was a major center for trade. Thousands of ships passed through its port. While some brought treasures, others brought death and disease. Did a nearby island called Poveglia help save the people of Venice from this threat?

The island of Poveglia

Inside Poveglia's abandoned mental hospital

A horrible disease called plague hit Venice in 1576. This disease spreads quickly from person to person. Plague can cause someone to run a fever, bleed under their skin, cough up blood, and—often within a few days—it can kill them. During an outbreak in the 1500s, nearly a third of the people in Venice died.

Terrified, people looked for a way to stop the illness from spreading. One solution was to force victims of the disease to live on nearby islands, including Poveglia. It didn't take long, however, for the dead in these places to quickly outnumber the living. As many as 160,000 are said to have died on the island of Poveglia.

A plague mask found on the island

In 1922, a mental hospital was built on the island. According to reports, ghosts of plague victims soon haunted the patients—as well as the hospital's director. The director was said to have performed cruel experiments on his patients in order to try to cure them. He eventually became mentally ill and threw himself off the top of the island's church. According to legend, he survived the fall, only to be strangled by a ghostly mist when he reached the ground.

During the 1500s, some people believed that plague victims became vampires. To stop them from attacking people, gravediggers shoved stones or bricks into the mouths of corpses.

The Tree of Tears

PEORIA STATE HOSPITAL
BARTONVILLE, ILLINOIS

Many of the patients at Peoria State Hospital spent most of their lives there. It was the only home they knew. Some who died at the hospital were buried there, too. They were often mourned by a man who some say still lives there—even after his own death.

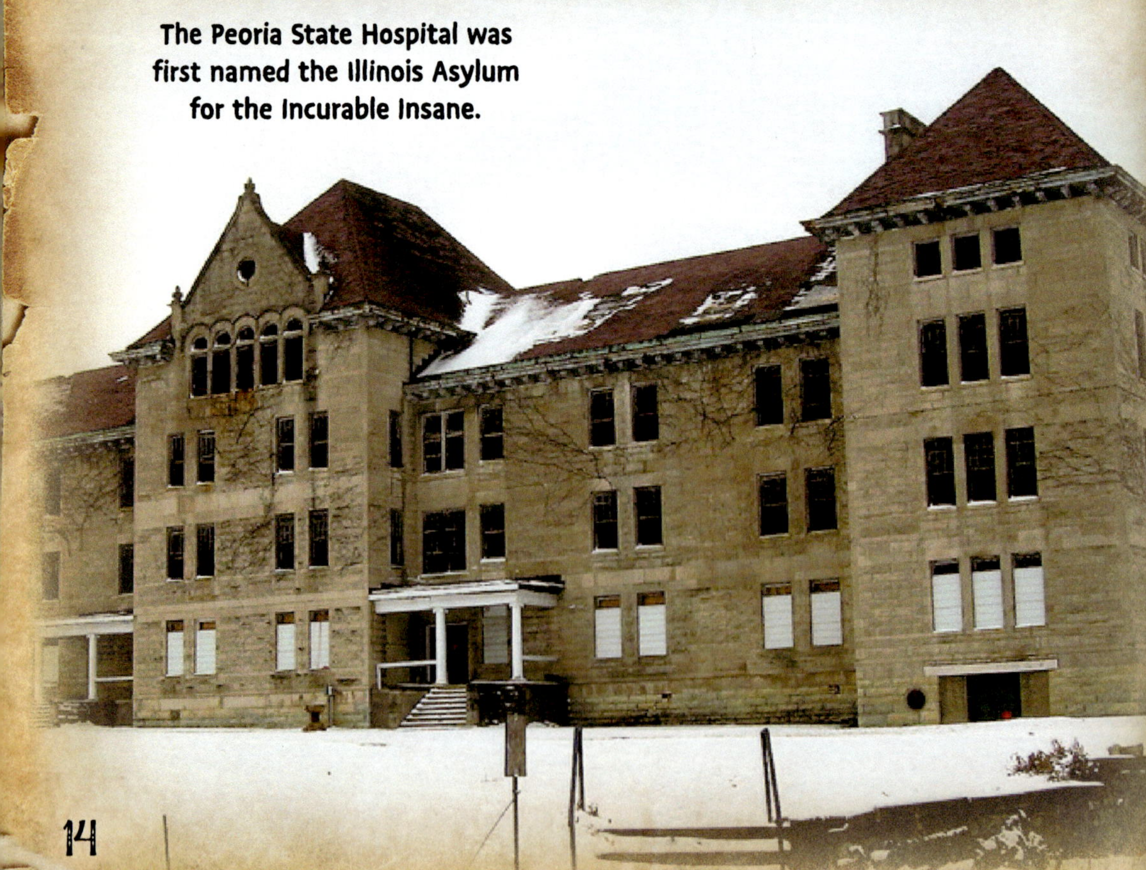

The Peoria State Hospital was first named the Illinois Asylum for the Incurable Insane.

In the early 1900s, a man called Bookbinder was a patient at the Peoria State Hospital. Dr. George Zeller, who ran the hospital, had him work as a gravedigger at the hospital's cemetery.

Every time Bookbinder helped bury a patient, he would cry. Often, he would lean against an old elm tree as he sobbed.

When Bookbinder died in 1910, most of the staff attended his funeral. As they put his coffin into the ground, the staff heard a wail coming from the old elm. People turned to find out who had made the noise. Next to the tree, they saw Bookbinder, crying his eyes out.

Was the dead man no longer in his coffin? Dr. Zeller quickly opened it to see, but Bookbinder's body was still inside. When people looked back at the elm, his ghost had disappeared.

The old elm at Peoria State Hospital began to die soon after Bookbinder's funeral. When workmen started chopping down the dying tree, they heard a cry of pain. So, they tried burning the tree instead. At the sound of sobbing, they quickly put out the flames.

Abused and Abandoned

PENNHURST STATE SCHOOL AND HOSPITAL
SPRING CITY, PENNSYLVANIA

In 1908, Pennhurst State School and Hospital opened to help care for people with mental and physical disabilities. Unfortunately, the hospital did not have enough money or workers to help the thousands of patients crowded into the building. Many died. According to some, their ghosts still haunt the hospital that was once their home.

Pennhurst State School and Hospital

In 1946, there were only 7 doctors serving more than 2,000 patients at Pennhurst State School and Hospital. By 1955, there were about 3,500 patients. Because there were so few people on staff, many patients were forced to spend their days and nights locked in metal cribs. Others wandered around naked because no one would help them get dressed.

When the staff tried to control patients, they often went too far. They broke patients' bones and knocked out their teeth with their rough handling. To stop the mistreatment, the hospital was closed in 1987.

Pennhurst has had such a sad and disturbing history, how could the spirits of troubled patients not linger there? Some people who have visited the abandoned hospital say they have heard voices in the narrow, dark tunnels that connect the buildings. Others have heard screams and slamming doors. Even those who haven't heard anything still have had the uneasy feeling of being watched.

A bed in the abandoned hospital

Terri Lee Halderman spent 11 years at Pennhurst. During her time there, she lost several teeth and had broken fingers and toes. She also received numerous cuts, scratches, and bites.

Lost But Not Forgotten

ATHENS MENTAL HEALTH CENTER
ATHENS, OHIO

Around three million soldiers fought in the U.S. Civil War (1861–1865). After the war ended, many of the men suffered from nightmares and painful memories. At times, their problems were overwhelming. Several huge asylums were built to help treat them and other patients. Some of the buildings were so big that a person could easily become lost in them.

Today, part of the Athens Mental Health Center is an art museum.

On December 1, 1978, one of the patients at Athens Mental Health Center disappeared. Her name was Margaret Schilling. A search party was formed to find her. They looked in each of the huge building's 544 rooms. Yet they found no trace of Margaret.

Weeks later, a janitor made a shocking discovery. Margaret was found dead in the attic. Unable to care for herself, Margaret probably died from starvation or from the cold temperatures in the unheated room.

Margaret's body was removed, but a detailed outline of it remained on the marble floor. The folds of her clothes and the style of her hair could easily be seen. The floor was cleaned over and over again, but the stain wouldn't go away. It can still be seen there today.

A fountain on the grounds of the Health Center

Due to overcrowding at Athens in the early 1900s, many patients were forced to sleep together in rooms meant for one person. As they lay there hour after hour, some would carve messages on their windowsills. One that can still be seen reads, "I was never crazy."

Left to Die

KALAUPAPA LEPER COLONY
ISLAND OF MOLOKA'I, HAWAII

Leprosy is a disease that attacks a person's nerves, skin, and eyes. Before a cure was found, many people who had it were quarantined so that they couldn't spread the disease to others. One place they were sent was to the Kalaupapa leper colony on the island of Moloka'i (mah-luh-KYE), Hawaii. Few who were forced to live there ever left.

The Kalaupapa leper colony on Moloka'i

The island of Moloka'i

On January 6, 1866, a dozen people who were suffering from leprosy were dropped off on the rocky island of Moloka'i, Hawaii. They were given only a few shovels and axes, wool blankets, some beef, bread, and two cottages to live in. Each week, ships brought more victims of the disease.

For years, doctors at the small hospital on the island could do nothing more to help their patients than change their bandages. When examining the wounds of a leper, one doctor used his cane—rather than his hands—to lift up the victim's bandages. He was afraid that if he touched his patients he would catch the disease himself.

Leprosy victims from countries around the world, including the United States, China, Spain, England, France, Korea, and Japan, were sent to the Kalaupapa colony. Between 1866 and 1969, more than 8,000 victims were torn from their families and forced to live on the island. About half were between the ages of 11 and 25.

Today, leprosy is known as Hansen's disease. It begins with a rash that slowly spreads over a person's body and causes a loss of feeling in the skin. Fingers and toes may curl up as hands and feet become weak. Doctors now have medicines to cure Hansen's disease.

People who lived at the Kalaupapa colony

The Scary Sounds of Soft Walls

FREMANTLE LUNATIC ASYLUM
FREMANTLE, AUSTRALIA

Violent patients at asylums were often placed in special cells. These rooms had no furniture. The walls and floors were covered with soft padding to stop patients from harming themselves on hard or sharp edges. The Fremantle Lunatic Asylum had one such padded cell for its most difficult inmates. Although the asylum was closed more than 100 years ago, some say the cell may not be empty.

Fremantle Lunatic Asylum

Visitors to the Fremantle History Museum can easily see signs of the gloomy building's original use. Past a thick wooden door lies the former asylum's padded cell. Bars line the room's window. Visitors can still see the peephole on the door that doctors used to spy on their patients.

Built by prisoners in the 1860s, the former lunatic asylum is considered one of Australia's most haunted places. The creepy padded cell where the most violent patients were kept has frightened more than one visitor. A local historian who toured it heard the voice of a young woman screaming. When her friend touched the door, the voice screamed, "Don't shut it!" She listened to the voice and left the door open.

Padded cells were also called rubber rooms.

Horror Movie Hospital

LINDA VISTA HOSPITAL
LOS ANGELES, CALIFORNIA

This hospital in Los Angeles, California, was once one of the best in the country. Now, some people say Linda Vista is one of the best places to find ghosts.

The abandoned Linda Vista Hospital

The Linda Vista Hospital was first established in 1904 for railroad employees. Workers who had diseases such as tuberculosis or who were injured on the job went to the hospital for first-class treatment. As the years passed, however, the hospital steadily declined.

With little money to run the hospital, the staff could no longer provide care to the sick in addition to all the victims of gunshots and stabbings that came through its doors. In 1991, the last patient checked out of Linda Vista, and the hospital was shut down.

Since then, ghost hunters have found many spirits in the building. Some claim to have heard a little girl crying for help from the fifth floor. Others have seen a doctor who roams the corridors. There is also a strange green light that appears at night from some of the windows.

The hospital is so frightening that it has been the setting for a number of horror movies. One film crew member said, "Everything is fine in most of the building, but there are places where the air suddenly changes. There's a feeling that if I go any further—if I keep walking in that direction—something's going to get me."

According to some, the ghosts at Linda Vista smash locks, break windows, and knock down doors.

Murder at the Metropolitan

METROPOLITAN STATE HOSPITAL
WALTHAM, MASSACHUSETTS

Large asylums cared for many types of mentally ill patients. Some patients heard voices when no one was talking. Others believed they saw things that weren't really there. A small number were even capable of murder. Such was the case with Melvin Wilson.

Metropolitan State Hospital

On August 9, 1978, patient Anne Marie Davee was granted a pass to walk around Metropolitan State Hospital. When she didn't return, the grounds were searched. Doctors assumed she had wandered off. Months passed with no sign of her. Hospital workers did, however, find her purse. It contained sunglasses and photographs. There was also a small axe inside!

The police soon realized how the axe was connected to Anne Marie. A fellow patient, Melvin Wilson, had used it to kill her. He had chopped up her body and buried it in three shallow graves near the hospital. He had also kept seven of Anne Marie's teeth. On August 12, 1980, Wilson led investigators to her body. He was later charged with murder and sent to another mental hospital.

A children's center at the hospital

In the early 1960s, children suffering from mental illness were treated at Metropolitan. It is rumored that the doctors accidentally poisoned more than two dozen of them. They had put a chemical in the children's milk, believing it would treat their illness. It killed them instead.

World War II Ghosts

OLD CHANGI HOSPITAL
CHANGI VILLAGE, SINGAPORE

Down the dark, narrow streets of Changi (CHANG-ee) Village lies the abandoned Old Changi Hospital. Once a military hospital, it is now considered by some to be the most haunted spot in one of Asia's most ghost-filled cities.

Old Changi Hospital

During World War II (1939–1945), the Japanese invaded the island of Singapore. During the three years they controlled the country, from 1942 to 1945, the Japanese were cruel to its citizens. They killed as many as 50,000 people who were thought to be anti-Japanese. More than 7,000 prisoners of war were crammed into the small prison in Changi Village.

In the 1930s, a hospital had been built in Changi. During the Japanese invasion, however, it was turned into a place of great suffering. The Japanese secret police were said to have set up a torture chamber in the building. They used pain to get information from prisoners about their country's war plans.

In 1997, the Old Changi Hospital was shut down when a newer hospital was built nearby. But according to some, reminders of the hospital's painful past remain. The ghosts of the victims are sometimes spotted at the abandoned hospital—often missing their heads and feet.

Inside Old Changi Hospital

In 2010, a film crew visited Old Changi Hospital. They hoped to prove that the abandoned building was haunted. It didn't take long to do so. One night soon after filming began, a terrifying ghostlike figure was said to have appeared. The crew ran out of the hospital in fear.

Trapped by Fire

SEACLIFF LUNATIC ASYLUM
SEACLIFF, NEW ZEALAND

During World War II, many nurses left their jobs at mental hospitals to care for wounded soldiers. This left some asylums with a much smaller staff than they needed. So, what happens when there is an emergency at a mental hospital and there aren't enough workers? In 1942, the patients of Seacliff Lunatic Asylum found out.

Seacliff Lunatic Asylum

On December 9, 1942, the female patients in Ward 5 of the Seacliff Lunatic Asylum were locked in their rooms for the night. There was a shortage of nurses at the hospital, so none were on duty that evening. At 9:45 p.m., a male worker finally noticed that the wooden building was in flames. The hospital firefighters battled the fierce blaze. However, they were only able to save two patients. After an hour, Ward 5 was a pile of smoking ashes, and 37 women were dead.

The fire, one of the worst in New Zealand's history, damaged only one building at Seacliff. So, the asylum was able to continue caring for its patients. The treatment there, however, was as cruel as it was at other asylums of the time. Patients were beaten and given lobotomies. While many tried to run away, the asylum kept taking in new patients.

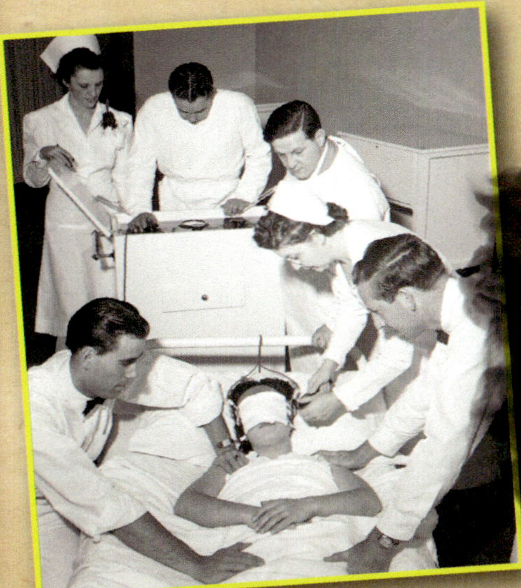

A patient receiving electroshock therapy in the 1940s

Electroshock therapy was widely used at Seacliff. This treatment, developed in the 1930s, involves sending an electric current through a patient's brain. Although electroshock therapy was misused in the past, doctors today think it can, in fact, help some people.

The Trail of Typhoid Mary

RIVERSIDE HOSPITAL
NORTH BROTHER ISLAND, NEW YORK

Although millions of people live in New York City today, no one makes a home on the city's North Brother Island. Yet for more than 75 years, the island's hospital was a place where many people came to stay—until they died.

Mary Mallon

Riverside Hospital's tuberculosis building

In 1885, Riverside Hospital was opened to care for victims of deadly diseases, including smallpox, typhus, and tuberculosis. During the 1892 typhus outbreak, New Yorkers who showed symptoms were immediately put on a ferry and sent to the hospital. Many never returned. About 1,200 people were quarantined at Riverside to try and stop the spread of the disease.

Over the years, the most famous of all the patients at Riverside was Mary Mallon, a cook better known as Typhoid Mary. Although she had typhoid fever, she didn't feel sick. As a result, Mary didn't believe she was spreading the disease and refused to stop working. During her lifetime, Mary is known to have infected at least 47 people. In the early 1900s, health authorities finally tracked her down and forced her to stay at Riverside Hospital. She spent 26 years there, until her death in 1938.

Dead bodies on North Brother Island after the ferry accident

In 1904, an overcrowded ferry called the *General Slocum* burst into flames in New York's East River. With rotted life jackets and useless lifeboats, it ran aground on North Brother Island. Nurses and doctors from Riverside Hospital rushed into the water to help. Still, more than 1,000 people died.

Taking the Care out of Caring

WHITTINGHAM HOSPITAL
WHITTINGHAM, ENGLAND

Like many asylums in the 1800s, Whittingham was created to care for the mentally ill. Unlike other asylums, it had its own train station, brass band, orchestra, post office, and church. How did a place so thoughtfully designed turn into a place so unfeeling?

Whittingham Hospital

In 1967, a collection of articles and essays called *Sans Everything* was published. The book described the cruel ways mentally ill patients were treated at asylums. The author could easily have been describing life at Whittingham. The rooms in this asylum were damp and cold. They were crawling with cockroaches and ants. Some patients were locked in small rooms or bathrooms. Others were left outside, regardless of the weather.

The staff would sometimes beat patients and tie them to chairs. Workers calmed down patients using what was known as the wet towel treatment. This involved twisting a wet towel around a patient's neck until they passed out. Nurses were even accused of setting one patient's clothes on fire—while they were still being worn!

Whittingham had a lot of activities for patients, and it looked lovely. Without a caring staff, however, it was just a pretty prison.

The inside of Whittingham after it was abandoned

During World War II, Whittingham had more than 3,000 patients. This made it the largest asylum in England at that time.

Fresh Air, Sunshine, and Death

WAVERLY HILLS SANATORIUM
LOUISVILLE, KENTUCKY

Tuberculosis is a terrifying illness that attacks a person's lungs. People who suffer from the deadly disease have chest pain and trouble breathing. They may even cough up blood. Before effective medicines were developed in the 1940s, many victims hoped that special tuberculosis hospitals called sanatoriums would save them. Sadly, many of those people ended up dead.

Waverly Hills Sanatorium

Waverly Hills was a huge sanatorium built on a hill in Louisville, Kentucky. The hospital opened in 1926. Tuberculosis patients who stayed there hoped the fresh air, sunshine, and rest that Waverly Hills provided would save them. Unfortunately for most, it didn't. Before the tuberculosis hospital closed in 1961, around 6,000 patients are believed to have died there.

When the disease was at its worst, someone died nearly every day at Waverly Hills. Those who worked at the hospital needed a way to transport the dead bodies without upsetting the patients who were trying to get well. So, they used rail cars that secretly traveled down a 500-foot (150-m) tunnel from the hospital to hearses waiting below. The pitch-black tunnel soon became known as the body chute.

When so many people die in one place, some believe their spirits are bound to remain. Stories say that in 1928, the head nurse in Room 502 killed herself. Her sad spirit is thought by some to still haunt the empty building.

The Battle to Live

CAMP LETTERMAN GENERAL HOSPITAL
GETTYSBURG, PENNSYLVANIA

One of the bloodiest battles in history was fought during the U.S. Civil War. For three days in July 1863, more than 150,000 soldiers clashed in Gettysburg, Pennsylvania, with around 50,000 killed, wounded, or missing. For many of these injured soldiers, Camp Letterman General Hospital was just a brief stop on their way to the graveyard.

Camp Letterman General Hospital

The Battle of Gettysburg

Following the horror of the Battle of Gettysburg, thousands of wounded soldiers were sent by trains to hospitals. However, nearly 5,000 soldiers were too badly injured to be moved. On July 22, 1863, a hospital called Camp Letterman was set up on the battlefield to care for the patients where they were.

A wounded Civil War soldier

There, 500 tents were filled with the sick and wounded. According to one nurse, "shrieks, cries, and groans" could be heard all around. "Not only from those in the tents," she added, "but on the amputating tables, which were almost constantly occupied." If surgery didn't kill the soldiers, infections or diarrhea often did. Ghosts of the many soldiers who failed to survive have been spotted on the battlefield. The ghost of a young, legless man appears to guests at a motel that was built over a site of heavy fighting. Today, Gettysburg is considered one of the most haunted places in America.

At the time of the Civil War, medicines that could stop infections in wounds had not yet been developed. Instead of treating wounds on a limb, doctors often simply cut off the injured arm or leg using saws and knives.

A Haunted Hospital

THE SPANISH MILITARY HOSPITAL MUSEUM
ST. AUGUSTINE, FLORIDA

St. Augustine, Florida, was founded in 1565 by Spanish explorers. The hospital that was built there in 1784, the Royal Hospital of Our Lady of Guadalupe, was a temporary home to those injured in clashes with Native Americans or in wars. Some say the site is now a permanent home to many ghosts.

Spanish Military Hospital Museum

The Royal Hospital of Our Lady of Guadalupe was torn down in 1821. Years later, the Spanish Military Hospital Museum was built on the site to show visitors what it was like to be a patient there in 1791. The tour visits the mourning room, where patients were blessed by a priest moments before they died. It also shows the surgery room, where cutting off an arm or a leg was often the only way to save a life.

While visitors learn about the hospital's history, they may also meet some of the ghosts that have been haunting this building for many years. Some people who have visited the mourning room have claimed the bed looked like someone was lying on it—but no one was there. According to reports from visitors, other beds have been pushed across rooms by unseen hands. The sounds of footsteps, moans, and sobbing have come from empty rooms. The many ghosts have also reportedly touched, pushed, and even bitten unsuspecting visitors.

In 1821, workers demolished the hospital to put in new water pipes for the city. Buried deep under the building were piles of human bones. It is now believed that the hospital was built over an old Native American burial site. Some believe this is another reason the area is so haunted.

A World of . . .

A wailing gravedigger in Bartonville, Illinois

A phantom nurse in Louisville, Kentucky

A body outline in Athens, Ohio

A cruel doctor in Kansas City, Missouri

A murder victim in Waltham, Massachusetts

A crying girl in Los Angeles, California

A trail of death on North Brother Island, New York

NORTH AMERICA

Mistreated patients in Spring City, Pennsylvania

PACIFIC OCEAN

ATLANTIC OCEAN

Civil War spirits in Gettysburg, Pennsylvania

An abandoned colony in Moloka'i, Hawaii

A military hospital in St. Augustine, Florida

SOUTH AMERICA

SOUTHERN OCEAN

Horror Healing

ARCTIC OCEAN

Abused residents in Whittingham, England

A Roman specter in Derby, England

ASIA

A bedlam hospital in London, England

EUROPE

A plague island in Poveglia, Italy

PACIFIC OCEAN

World War II ghosts in Changi Village, Singapore

AFRICA

INDIAN OCEAN

The padded cell in Fremantle, Australia

AUSTRALIA

A devastating fire in Seacliff, New Zealand

Glossary

abandoned left empty or no longer used

amputating tables tables on which a person's arm or a leg is cut off for medical reasons

asylums hospitals that take care of people who are mentally ill

bandages pieces of cloth that are wrapped around injured parts of a body

cemetery an area of land where dead bodies are buried

Civil War the war in the United States between the northern and southern states that lasted from 1861 until 1865

cloak a loose coat with no sleeves that hangs over the shoulders, arms, and back

coffin a container in which a dead person is placed for burial

corpses dead bodies

disabilities conditions that make it hard for people to do everyday things, such as walking, seeing, or hearing

eye socket a bony hole in the skull that surrounds and protects the eyeball

graves holes dug in the ground where dead people are buried

hearses cars that carry coffins to be buried

ice pick a sharp tool used for chipping away at chunks of ice

infections illnesses caused by germs entering the body

inmates people who are forced to live in an asylum or prison

insane mentally ill

legend a story that is handed down from the past that may be based on fact but is not always completely true

linger to remain longer than expected

lobotomies surgical procedures meant to calm violent people; a sharp instrument is forced into the brain through the eye socket in order to cut some of the nerve connections in the patient's brain

lunatics a term that is used to describe mentally ill people in a negative way

mental hospital a medical facility that takes care of people who have a sickness that impacts how their brain works

mentally ill having a sickness that impacts how the brain works

morgue a place where dead bodies are kept before being buried

mourned felt very sad over someone who died

Native Americans the indigenous peoples of North America, especially in the United States

nerve one of the many fibers that sends messages between a person's brain and other parts of their body

paranormal events that are not able to be scientifically explained

peephole a small hole through which a person secretly looks at something

plague a deadly disease that is spread by fleas and rodents

port a place where ships load and unload goods

quarantined separated from other people in order to prevent the spread of a disease

sanatoriums buildings where patients suffering from certain long-term diseases stay to improve their health and ease symptoms

spirits supernatural creatures

starvation the act of dying from lack of food

strangled choked to death

surgery the part of medical science that treats injuries or diseases by fixing or removing parts of the body

symptoms signs of a disease or other physical problem felt by a person

tuberculosis a disease that usually affects the lungs and causes fever, coughing, and difficulty breathing

typhoid fever a disease spread by bacteria that can cause fever, diarrhea, weakness, and headaches

typhus any one of a group of diseases spread by fleas, lice, and mites that cause fever and weakness

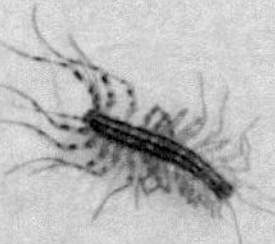

Read More

Sheen, Barbara. *Ghosts and Spirits (Exploring the Occult)*. San Diego, CA: ReferencePoint Press, 2024.

Snowden, Matilda & Joyce Markovics. *Investigating Ghosts in Hospitals (Investigating Ghosts)*. Hallandale Beach, FL: Mitchell Lane Publishers, 2021.

Spilsbury, Louise. *Ghosts and Haunted Places: Investigating History's Mysteries (Spooked!)*. Shrewsbury, Shropshire: Cheriton Children's Books, 2024.

Troupe, Thomas Kingsley. *Haunted Hospitals and Asylums (The Haunted!)*. New York: Crabtree Publishing Company, 2022.

Learn More Online

1. Go to **www.factsurfer.com** or scan the QR code below.

2. Enter "**Horror Healing**" into the search box.

3. Click on the cover of this book to see a list of websites.

Index

Where do you
dare NOT go?